# The Forest of Vazon: A Guernsey Legend of the Eighth Century

Anonymous

# THE FOREST OF VAZON

*A GUERNSEY LEGEND OF THE EIGHTH CENTURY.*

1889.

Old House of the Haye du Puits, Guernsey. Sketched in 1838.

# PREFACE.

Nothing authentic is known of the history of Guernsey previously to its annexation to the Duchy of Normandy in the tenth century. The only sources of information as to events which may have occurred before that date are references in monkish chronicles of the usual semi-mythical type, and indications conveyed by cromlechs and menhirs, fragments of Celtic instruments and pottery, and a few Roman relics. It is unfortunate that we are thus precluded from acquiring any knowledge of the development of a people as to whom the soundest among conflicting conjectures seems to be that, coming originally from Brittany, they preserved the purity of the Celtic race through periods when in other offshoots of the same stock its characteristics were being obliterated by the processes of crossing and absorption.

If early local records had existed they would hardly have failed to have given minute details of the convulsion of nature which resulted in the destruction by the sea of the forest lands on the northern and western sides of the island, and in the separation of tracts of considerable magnitude from the mainland. Geologists are agreed in assigning to this event the date of March, 709, when great inundations occurred in the Bay of Avranches on the French coast; they are not equally unanimous as to the cause, but science now rejects the theory of a raising of the sea-level and that of a general subsidence of the island. The most reasonable explanation appears to be that the overpowering force of a tidal wave suddenly swept away barriers whose resistance had been for ages surely though imperceptibly diminishing, and that the districts thus left unprotected proved to be below the sea-level—owing, as regards the forests, to gradual subsidence easily explicable in the case of undrained, swampy soil; and, as regards the rocks, to the fact that the newly exposed surface consisted of accumulations of already disintegrated deposits.

It is unquestionable that before the inroad of the sea the inlet in the south-west of the island known as Rocquaine Bay was enclosed by two arms, the northern of which terminated in the point of Lihou; on which still stand the ruins of an old priory, while the southern ended in the Hanois rocks, on which a lighthouse has been erected. Lihou is at present an island, accessible only at low water by a narrow causeway; the Hanois is entirely cut off from the shore, but it is a noteworthy fact that the signs of old cart-ruts are visible at spring tides, and that an iron hook was recently discovered attached to a submerged rock which had apparently served as a gatepost; besides these proofs of the existence of roads now lying under the waves, it is said that an old order for the repair of Hanois roads is still extant. That Vazon and the Braye du Valle were the sites of forests is indisputable, though the former is now a sandy bay into which the Atlantic flows without hindrance, and the latter, reclaimed within the present century by an enterprising governor, formed for centuries a channel of the sea by which the Clos du Valle, on which the Vale Church stands, was separated from the mainland. A stratum of peat extends over the whole arm of the Braye, while as regards Vazon there is the remarkable evidence of an occurrence which took place in December, 1847. A strong westerly gale, blowing into the bay concurrently with a low spring tide, broke up the bed of peat and wood underlying the sand and gravel, and lifted it up like an ice-floe; it was then carried landwards by the force of the waves. The inhabitants flocked to the spot, and the phenomenon was carefully inspected by scientific observers. Trunks of full-sized trees were seen, accompanied by meadow plants and roots of rushes and weeds, surrounded by those of grasses and mosses; the perfect state of the trees showed that they had been long buried under the sand. Some of the trees and boughs were at first mistaken for wreckage, but the fishermen soon discovered their error and loaded their carts with the treasure locally known as "gorban." Subsequent researches have shown that acorns and hazel-nuts, teeth of horses and hogs, also pottery and instruments of the same character as those found in the cromlechs, exist among the Vazon peat deposits. There is therefore abundant evidence that the legends relating to the former inhabitants of the forest are based on traditions resting on an historical foundation.

CONTENTS.

PREFACE.

ILLUSTRATIONS

ILLUSTRATIONS.

# CHAPTER I.

## TRADITION.

"What can he tell that treads thy shore?
No legend of thine olden time,
No theme on which the mind might soar
High as thine own in days of yore."

*The Giaour.*—BYRON

In the beginning of the eighth century Guernsey was a favoured spot. Around, over the Continent and the British Isles, had swept successive conquests with their grim train of sufferings for the conquered; but these storm-clouds had not burst over the island. The shocks which preceded the fall of the Roman Empire had not been felt, nor had the throes which inaugurated the birth of Frankish rule in Gaul and Saxon supremacy in Britain, disturbed the prevailing tranquillity. Occasional descents of pirates, Northmen from Scandinavian homes or Southmen from the Iberian peninsula, had hitherto had a beneficial effect by keeping alive the martial spirit and the vigilance necessary for self-defence. In the third century three Roman ships had been driven on shore and lost; the legionaries who escaped had established themselves in the island, having indeed for the moment no alternative. When their commander succeeded in communicating with Gaul he suggested a permanent occupation, being secretly influenced by tales of mineral wealth to which he had lent an ear. Disillusioned and recalled, he was followed by a sybarite, whose palate was tickled by banquets of fish of which he wrote in raptures to his friends at Capri and Brindisi. This excellent man, dying of apoplexy in his bath, was replaced by a rough soldier, who lost no time in procuring the evacuation of a post where he saw with a glance that troops were uselessly locked up. From this time nothing had been heard of the Romans; their occupation had lasted forty years, and in another forty the only physical traces of it remaining were a camp at Jerbourg, the nearly obliterated tessellated pavement and fragments of wall belonging to the sybarite's villa, which occupied the site in the King's Mills Valley where the Moulin

1

de Haut now stands, the pond in the Grand Mare in which the voluptuary had reared the carp over which, dressed with sauces the secret of which died with him, he dwelt lovingly when stretched on his triclinium, and the basins at Port Grat in which he stored his treasured mullet and succulent oysters. The islanders were of one mind in speeding the parting guests, but the generation which saw them go were better men than their fathers who had trembled at the landing of the iron-thewed demi-gods. Compelled to work as slaves, they had learnt much from their masters; a knowledge of agriculture and of the cultivation of the grape, the substitution of good weapons and implements of husbandry for those of their Celtic ancestors, improved dwellings, and some insight into military discipline,— these were substantial benefits which raised them in some respects above their Continental and British neighbours, among whom patriotism had, on the disappearance of the civilization of the Romans, revived the more congenial barbarism. Arrivals among them of Christian monks, scanty at first, more frequent since the landing of S. Augustine in Britain, had also had a certain effect. The progress of conversion was, however, slow; the people were bigoted, and the good fathers were compelled, as in Brittany, to content themselves with a few genuine converts, wisely endeavouring rather to leaven the mass by grafting Christian truths on the old superstitions than to court certain defeat, possible expulsion or massacre, by striving to overthrow at once all the symbols of heathenism.

The island was larger in extent than it is at present, as, in addition to the Vale district, the islet of Lihou, Vazon Bay, and the rock group known as the Hanois formed part of it. It is with the events that altered this configuration that the following legend deals.

## CHAPTER II.

## SUPERSTITION.

"Awestruck, the much-admiring crowd
Before the virgin vision bowed,
Gaz'd with an ever-new delight,
And caught fresh virtues at the sight."

EDWARD MOORÉ'S *Fables*.

On the 24th of June, in the year 708, merry crowds were thronging to Vazon Forest. It was a lovely spot. The other portions of the island were bare and somewhat rugged; here the humidity of the soil favoured the growth of fine, vigorous timber. On the low ground flourished oak and sycamore, torn and bent near the shore where the trees met the force of the Atlantic gales, growing freely and with rich verdure where better protected. On the higher slopes were massed beech, birch, and the sweet chestnut which was even then domesticated in the island. Glades, bursting with a wealth of flowers nurtured by the mildness of the climate, penetrated the wood in every direction; streams bubbling up from springs, and forming little cascades where their course was checked by granite boulders, lent an additional charm. Towards the centre of the forest these streams united to form a lake, or rather a natural moat, surrounding an island in the midst of which stood a gigantic oak. This was the only tree on the island; round it, at even distances, were placed twelve stones, beyond which a meadow glittering with varied hues extended to the surrounding water.

It was to this island that the holiday-makers were wending their way: young men and maidens, and such elders as had vigour enough to traverse the rough tracks leading from the interior. They were a small race, lithe and active, with strong black hair and dark eyes now twinkling with merriment They poured over the wooden bridges into the precincts of the towering oak, under which the elders seated themselves with the musicians, the younger people streaming off to the clear ground between the stones and the water.

When all were assembled the music struck up at a signal from an elder. The instruments were akin to the goat-skin pipes of Lower Brittany; the music wild, weird, appealing to the passion if not melodious to the ear. At any rate the effect was inspiriting. First, the men danced, the maidens seating themselves round the dancers and chanting the following words, to the rhythm of which they swayed their bodies gracefully:—

> "Mille Sarrazins, mille Sarmates,
> Un jour nous avons tués.
> Mille, mille, mille, mille, mille Perses,
> Nous cherchons à present."

The dance, footed to this truculent chant, had no warlike features; beginning with a march, or rather a tripping walk, it ended with feats in which each dancer defied his neighbour to out-spring him; nor did the vocalists appear to expect representations of strife and doughty deeds. The words, Roman by origin, as is clear from the allusion to the Persians, had been adapted to a native air by the conquerors, and had been left by them as a legacy to the islanders. Next, the maidens trod a measure, the men standing round and applauding; the dance was quiet and soft, consisting principally of graceful movements of the body as if the dancers were getting themselves into training for greater efforts; in this case the dancers themselves chanted words suitable to the music. This ended, there was a pause before the principal business of the day began, the dance in which both sexes joined, to be followed by the bestowal of a wreath on the loveliest of the maidens.

During the pause it was evident that an unusual incident had occurred. The best-looking of the girls were pouting, the attention of the youths was distracted. During the latter part of the dance the applause had been intermittent; towards the close it had almost ceased. The elders, looking about under their shaggy eyebrows, had not been long in discovering the cause, and when they had found it allowed their attention to wander also.

The disturbing element was, indeed, not far to seek. Close to one of the bridges was seated a maiden, unknown to all of them, but lovely enough to hold the glance of old and young. Unlike the natives she

4

was tall and fair; masses of golden hair encircled her oval face and clustered over her blue eyes. Who was she? Whence came she? None could answer. By degrees some of the boldest of the youths approached, but their bluff manners seemed to displease her; though unaccustomed to rebuffs they retired. One, however, among them fared differently. Jean Letocq, a member of the family to which the hero belonged who near this very spot discovered the sleeping troops of the Grand Sarrazin, was admired and beloved both by youths and maidens. First in every sport, having shown courage and resource in times of peril both by sea and land, tender of glance and gentle of tongue, he held a pre-eminence which none disputed, and which was above the reach of envy. The fair stranger, from his first glance at her, had fascinated, enthralled him: his eyes fastened greedily on her every movement; he noted well her reception of those who had addressed her, and when he approached he came, bare-headed, with a low obeisance and a deferential air. He seated himself by her in silence, after murmuring a few words of welcome to the feast, to which she made no answer. Presently he spoke again, softly and courteously; she replied without constraint, speaking his own language fluently, though with a foreign accent. The ice once broken their talk rippled on, as is the wont of light words, brightly uttered. Jean drank in each gentle phrase, watched every graceful gesture; his heart bounded when she carelessly smiled. But he lost not his daring: when the musicians again struck up he boldly asked her to join in the dance.

She was not offended, her look showed no displeasure, but she refused; he renewed his request; suddenly a change came over her face, she looked rapidly round as though searching for some one who was not present, a flash came into her eyes, she sprang to her feet. "Why should I not dance!" she said; "they are merry, why should I alone be sad!" She let him lead her into the ring. If she had been enchanting when seated, what was her power when she moved! She was a model of grace and loveliness; the contrast of her colouring to that of her neighbours inspired the superstitious with some terror, but made the braver spirits gaze more curiously, indifferent to the half-concealed anger and affected disdain of their partners. Every moment she gained more hearts, though she let her eyes rest only on those of Jean. After the dance was over she seated herself in her former position; the women then, according to custom, retired outside the stone circle, while the men clustered round the oak to award the prize. The ceremony had up to this day been looked on as a pure formality: for the last two summers the wreath had been by common consent placed on the brows of Suzanne Falla, and none who woke that morning had doubted that it would rest there again before night. But now the men's heads were turned; there was commotion both outside and inside the circle; then a hush, as the old men rose in their places and the young men formed a lane to the tree. Jean stepped out, and taking the stranger by the hand, led her to where a white-haired veteran stood with the wreath in his hand. The next moment it was placed on her brows, and then all voices burst into a song of triumph, which rang to the remotest glades of the forest. Suzanne did not join in the song; her little heart was breaking; all the passion of her hot nature was roused; she felt herself unfairly, unjustly, treated; insulted on the very day that was to have crowned her pride. She could not control herself, nor could she accept her defeat: she stamped her foot on the ground, and poured out a torrent of objurgation, accusing Jean of treachery, demanding to know whence he had produced her rival, appealing to the elders to revise the judgment. Then, suddenly ceasing, as she saw by the looks of those around her that while in some her fate created pity, in others it gave rise to amusement, in many to the pleasure which poor human nature felt then as now in a friend's misfortune, her mood altered: she turned and, rapidly leaving the crowd, crossed one of the bridges. Hastening her steps, but not watching them, she tripped over the straggling root of a yew, and fell, her temple striking a sharp boulder, one of many cropping up in the forest. Poor girl! in one moment passion and pride had flown; she lay senseless, blood streaming from the wound.

A quick revulsion of feeling swept through the impressionable people. Her departure had been watched, the fall observed, and the serious nature of the accident was soon known; all hurried to the spot where she lay, full of sympathy and distress. Jean, perhaps not altogether unremorseful, was among the first to proffer aid; the stranger, left alone, took off the wreath and placed it on one of the stones of the circle, by which she stood contemplating the scene.

The blow, struck deep into the temple, was beyond any ordinary means of cure; life indeed seemed to be ebbing away. "Send for Marie!" the cry sprang from many mouths: "send for Marie the wise woman! she alone can save her!" Three or four youths ran hastily off.

"Wish ye for Marie Torode's body or her spirit?" said a harsh female voice; "her body ye can have! but what avail closed eyes and rigid limbs? Her spirit, tossed by the whirling death-blast, is beyond your reach!"

The speaker, on whom all eyes turned, was an aged woman of unusual height; her snow-white hair was confined by a metal circlet, her eyes were keen and searching, her gestures imperious; her dress was simple and would have been rude but for the quaintly ornamented silver girdle that bound her waist, and the massive bracelets on her arms. Like the girl she was seen for the first time; her almost supernatural appearance inspired wonder and awe. She bent over the prostrate form: "Marie said with her last breath," she muttered to herself, "that ere the oaks were green again the sweetest maidens in the island would be in her embrace, but she cannot summon this one now! her vext spirit has not yet the power!"

She examined the wound, and raising herself said, "No human hand can save her. The Spirits alone have power: those Spirits who prolong human life regardless of human ills; but they must be besought, and who will care to beseech them?"

"Prayers may save her," answered a stern voice, "but not prayers to devils! The Holy Virgin should we beseech, by whom all pure maidens are beloved. She will save her if it be God's will, or receive her into her bosom if it be decreed that she should die."

The words were those of Father Austin, one of the monks of Lihou, distinguished by his sanctity and the austerity of his habits. He was spare, as one who lived hardly; his grey eyes had a dreamy look betokening much inward contemplation, though they could be keen enough when, as now, the man was roused; there was a gentleness about his mouth which showed a nature filled with love and sympathy.

The woman drew herself to her full stature, and turned on him a defiant look.

"Gods or devils!" she said in a ringing tone—"which you will! What can an immured anchorite know of the vast mysteries of the wind-borne spirits? Is this child to live or die? My gods can save her; if yours can, let them take her! She is nought to me."

"When Elijah wrestled with the prophets of Baal, where did victory rest?" said the priest, and he too stooped down and inspected the wound. "She is past cure," he said, rising sadly; "it remains but to pray for her soul."

At this critical moment an agonizing shriek rang through the forest. The same runners who had sped to Marie Torode's cottage and had learnt there that the wise woman had in truth passed away, had brought back with them Suzanne's mother, who threw herself on her child's body endeavouring to staunch the blood, and to restore animation. Finding her efforts vain, she had listened anxiously to the words that had passed, and on hearing the priest's sentence of doom she burst into frantic grief and supplication. Turning to each disputant she cried—"Save her! save her young life! I suckled her, I reared her, I love her!—oh, how I love her!—do not let her die!"

"She can be saved!" curtly responded the stranger. The priest was silent. A murmur arose. Austin, who had trained himself to study those among whom he laboured, saw that the feeling was rising strongly against him. His antagonist saw it also, and pressed her victory.

"Yes!" she said scornfully, "it is a small matter for my Gods to save her, but they will not be besought while this bald-pate obtrudes his presence. Let him leave us!"

The priest was much perplexed. He knew the skill of these lonely women; secretly he had faith in their power of witchcraft, though attributing it to the direct agency of Satan. He thought it not impossible that there was truth in the boast; and his heart was wrung with the mother's grief. On the other hand, the public defeat was a sore trial; but it was clear to him that for the present at least the analogy of Elijah's struggle was imperfect: he must wait, and meanwhile bear his discomfiture with meekness. He prepared to retire. The victor was not, however, even now satisfied. "Take with you," she said, "yon idol that defaces the sacred oak!"

The good fathers, following their usual practice of associating emblems of heathen with those of Christian worship, in the hope of gradually diverting the reverence to the latter without giving to the former a ruder shock than could be endured, had suspended a small cross on the oak, hoping eventually to carve the tree itself into a sacred emblem; it was to this that the woman was pointing with a sneer.

But this time she had made a blunder. Father Austin turned to the crucifix and his strength and fire returned. Taking it from the tree, reverently kissing it and holding it aloft, he said solemnly—"Let my brothers and sisters come with me! We will pray apart, where no profane words can reach us. Perchance our prayers may be granted!" Not a few of the hearers followed him; sufficient indeed to make an imposing procession: the triumph of the Evil One was at least dimmed.

But his adversary did not appear to notice their departure. She gave a sharp glance in the direction of the oak, and the now discrowned girl was quickly at her side. Receiving some rapid instructions, the latter disappeared into the wood, and shortly returned with some herbs, which she passed to her companion; she then resumed her position by the stone. The old woman placed some leaves, which she selected, on the wound: the bleeding at once ceased; squeezing juice from the herbs, she applied an ointment made from it; then, opening a phial attached to her waist-belt, she poured some drops of liquid into the girl's mouth, gently parting her lips. This done, she stood erect and began an incantation, or rather a supplication, in an unknown tongue. As she proceeded her form became rigid, her eye gleamed, her arms, the hands clenched, were raised above her head. The sun flashed on the circlet, glittered on the embossed girdle: on the right arm was a heavy bracelet, composed of a golden serpent winding in weird folds round a human bone; the head was towards the wearer's wrist, and the jewelled eyes which, being of large size, must have been formed of rare stones, glowed and shot fire as the red beams struck on them through the branches. It seemed that a forked tongue darted in and out, but this may have been imagined by the heated fancies of the bystanders. The prayer ended; the stillness of death rested a moment on man and nature; then a wild gust of wind, striking the oak without any preliminary warning, bent and snapped the upper branches, and crashed inland through the swaying forest. The watchers saw the colour return to the cheeks of the wounded girl, who opened her eyes and sate up. "Take her home," said the sorceress, now quite composed, to the mother; "she is yours again!—till Marie calls her!" she added in a low voice to herself. The happy mother, shedding tears of joy, but in vain attempting to get her thanks accepted, obeyed the injunction.

As she and her friends disappeared, the old woman, turning to the awed people who seemed more than ever disposed to look on her as a supernatural being, said sternly—"Why linger you here? Are you unmindful of your duties? See you not how the shadows lengthen?" These words produced a magical effect: the deep emotions by which the mass had been recently swayed were swiftly replaced by equally profound feelings of a different nature, as cloud succeeds cloud in a storm-swept sky.

And now a singular scene was enacted. A procession was formed, headed by the old men, bare-headed; the musicians followed, behind whom walked with solemn step the younger members of the community. This procession, emerging from the western border of the forest, slowly climbed the slopes of the Rocque du Guet, and arriving at the summit bent its way seaward, halting at the edge of the precipitous cliff.

The sun was nearing the horizon. The scene was one of unsurpassed loveliness. Behind lay the central and southern portions of the island, hushed as if their primaeval rocks were still tenantless. The outlines of the isles of Herm and Jethou were visible, but already sinking into the shades of evening. On the left the bold bluffs of L'Erée and Lihou, on the right the rugged masses of the Grandes and the Grosses Rocques, the Gros Commet, the Grande and Petite Fourque, lay in sharpened outline, the lapping waves already assuming a grey tint. These masses formed the framework of a picture which embraced a boundless wealth of colour, an infinite depth of softness. Straight from the sun shot out across Cobo Bay a joyous river of gold, so bright that eye could ill bear to face its glow; here and there in its course stood out quaintly-shaped rocks, some drenched with the fulness of the glorious bath, others catching now and again a sprinkling shower. On each side of the river the sea, clear to its depths where alternate sand and rock made a tangle of capriciously mingled light and shade; its surface, here blue as the still waters of the Grotta Azzurra, there green as the olive, here again red-brown as Carthaginian marble, lay waveless, as with a sense that the beauty was too perfect to be disturbed. Suddenly the scene was changed; the lustrous outflow was swiftly drawn in and absorbed; a grey hue swept over the darkening surface; in the distance the round, blood-coloured, orb hung above the expectant ocean.

Then all assembled fell on their knees. The music gave out sharp plaintive notes which were answered by the voices of men and women in short, wailing, as it were inquiring, rhythm; this continued till the sun was on the point of disappearance, when music and voices together burst into a sad chant, seemingly of farewell; the kneeling people extending their hands seaward with an appealing gesture. One figure only was erect; on the projecting boulder, which is still so conspicuous a feature of the Rocque du Guet, stood the sorceress, her arms also outstretched, her figure, firm, erect, sharply outlined, such as Turner's mind conceived when he sketched the Last Man.

Father Austin contemplated the scene from a distance. By his side was his favourite convert, Jean Letocq.

"Strange!" he said, placing his hand on his companion's shoulder. "Your race are not sun-worshippers. Never, except on this day of the year, do they show this feeling; but who that saw them to-day would doubt that they are so! Is it that from old times their intense love of nature has led them to show in this way their sadness at its decay? or do they by mourning over the close of the sun's longest day symbolize their recognition of the inevitable end of the longest life of man? I cannot tell. But, blind as this worship is, it is better than that of the work of man's hands. By God's will your countrymen may be led from kneeling to the created to mount the ladder till they bend the knee only to the Creator. It may be well, too, that their chosen object of veneration is the only object in nature which dies but to rise again. Thus may they be led to the comprehension of the great truth of the resurrection. But Satan," he added with warmth, "must be wrestled with and cast down, specially when he takes the forms of temptation which he has assumed to-day: those of power and beauty. Prayer and fasting are sorely needed."

For once his pupil was not altogether docile. "Thou hast taught me, father," he replied, "the lesson of charity. This old woman is sinful, her error is deep, but may she not be converted and saved?"

"The devils can never regain Paradise," replied the priest sternly. "Arm thyself, Jean, against their wiles, in which I fear thou art already entangled. The two forms we have to-day seen are but human in seeming: demons surely lurked beneath."

Jean was now in open rebellion. "Nay, good father," he said decisively, "the maiden was no fiend; if her companion be an imp of darkness, as well she may, be it my task to rescue her from the evil snare into which she has fallen!" He had indeed a vivid recollection of the soft, human hand to which he had ventured to give a gentle pressure when he had assisted in placing the wreath on the fair, marble, brow, and had no doubt of the girl's womanhood. As he spoke he vanished from the side of the priest, who, seeing the two objects of his pious aversion entering the darkening glades of the wood, was at no loss to divine the cause of his disappearance. The holy father shook his head, and sighed deeply. He was accustomed to disappointments, but this day his path had to an unusual extent been beset with thorns. His faith was unshaken, and he humbly laid the fault on his own shoulders, promising further privations to his already sorely afflicted body. Meanwhile he descended the hill, directing his course to Lihou. Pausing on his way through the forest to replace the cross on the oak, he saw Jean, walking slowly homewards, his listless step showing that his quest had failed. The Evil One had, he thought, for the time at least, forborne to press his advantage. Further off he heard the scattered voices of the dispersing throng.

CHAPTER III.

DEVOTION.

"There glides a step through the foliage thick,
And her cheek grows pale and her heart beats quick,
There whispers a voice through the rustling leaves,
And her blush returns, and her bosom heaves;
A moment more—and they shall meet.
'Tis past—her lover's at her feet."

*Parasina.*—BYRON.

After visiting all the accessible parts of the island Jean satisfied himself that it was useless to search further in them for traces of the strangers. Persons so remarkable could not, it was clear, conceal themselves from the knowledge of the inhabitants. He must therefore either admit that the monk's surmise was correct, or must search in quarters hitherto unexplored. Though his rejection of the former alternative was a foregone conclusion, his adoption of the latter was a remarkable proof of the strength of his passion. There was only one district unexplored, and that was practically unapproachable.

Early in the sixth century some piratical vessels had entered Rocquaine Bay in a shattered condition; the crews succeeded in landing, but the ships, for seagoing purposes, were beyond repair. The pirates penetrated inland, driving out the inhabitants from Torteval and some of the adjoining valleys. Here they settled; and being skilled in hunting and fishing, having a fair knowledge of husbandry, and finding the position peculiarly adapted for their marauding pursuits, throve and prospered: so much so that when, some years afterwards, they had an opportunity of leaving, the majority elected to remain. Their descendants had continued to occupy the same district. Who they were, whether pure Northmen or of some mixed race, it would be idle to conjecture: they were originally put down by the islanders as Sarrazins, that being the name under which the simple people classed all pirates; the strangers, however, resented this description, and had consequently come to be spoken of as Les Voizins, a definition to which no exception could be taken. Hardy and warlike, quick of temper and rough of speech, they had an undisputed ascendancy over the natives, to whom, though dangerous if provoked, they had often given powerful aid in times of peril. On the whole they made not bad neighbours, but a condition was imposed by them the violation of which was never forgiven: no native was permitted, under any pretext, to enter their territory; death was the sure fate of an intruder found in Rocquaine Bay or setting foot in the Voizin hills or valleys. Whatever may have been the cause of this regulation the result had been to keep the race as pure as it was on the day of the first landing.

Now it was in the Terre des Voizins that Jean had resolved to seek his beloved, and his resolution was unalterable. He knew the danger; he wished to avoid death if possible; he meant to employ to the full the resources at his command; foolhardy as his enterprise seemed it was long and carefully planned. He knew that in the summer evenings it was the custom of the Voizin women to visit the sunny shores of the bay: this he had seen from Lihou; could he then succeed in landing unperceived, and in concealing himself in one of the many clefts of the rocks, he felt sure that if the well-known form were there he would descry it; what would follow afterwards was a question which had taken many fantastic shapes in his imagination, none of which had assumed a definite form.

Towards the close of July the conditions were favourable for his attempt. In the night a strong tide would be running into the bay; the wind was south-westerly, the moon set early. He prepared to start. He had selected a small and light boat, which would travel fast under his powerful strokes, and might be so handled as not to attract attention; in it he had stored provisions which would last for a few days and a small cask of fresh water. Towards evening he shaped his course for Lihou.

He had seen but little of the monk since the day of the feast, but he was yearning to see him now. His love for the man, his reverence for the truths he taught, his thought of his own future if he lost his life in his rash expedition, all urged him to seek a parting interview.

The brothers received him affectionately and bade him join their frugal meal. The monks were five in number: they had been six, but one had recently been drowned while returning from a pious mission to Herm. Jean knew them all; they were honest, God-fearing men, trustful and truthful. If their reasoning powers were not great, their faith was unswerving. Their life was a prolonged asceticism, and they had fair reason to expect that martyrdom would be their earthly crown.

The only exceptional feature of the repast was the appearance of one who had never yet been seated there in Jean's presence; this guest was the hermit who dwelt on the extreme point, against which the Atlantic waves dashed in their fiercest fury. The recluse did not seem to cultivate the duty of abstemiousness, but he maintained silence. Jean could not forbear furtively scanning his appearance, which was indeed remarkable. He would have been of large stature in any country; compared with the natives his proportions were gigantic. His broad shoulders and muscular arms betokened enormous strength; his hair and beard were fair; his blue eyes had a clear, frank, expression; there was firmness of purpose in his massive jaw; he seemed between forty and fifty, and would have been strikingly handsome but for three deep scars which totally marred the expression of his features. As Jean eyed him he returned the compliment, but the meal was soon over and the youth accompanied Father Austin to his cell.

Roque du Guet and Cobo Bay. Sketched in 1839.

There a long and sleepless night was passed by both. The monk in vain endeavoured to combat Jean's resolution; he argued, prayed, indeed threatened, but without effect. Finding his efforts hopeless he abandoned them, and endeavoured to fortify his charge against the influence of the spell under which he believed him to have fallen. Then the young man was again the pupil; he listened humbly and reverently to the repetition of the great truths which the father strove to rivet on his mind, and joined earnestly in the prayers for truth and constancy. As daylight broke, and he at length laid himself down to rest, his latest vision was that of the good man kneeling by him with that rapt look of contemplation which seemed to foreshadow his immortality.

Jean slept profoundly for some hours. When night began to fall he received Austin's blessing, no further reference being made to his expedition, and when the moon was on the eve of disappearance he launched his boat. As he rounded Lihou point another boat shot out, the occupant of which hailed him. Recognizing the hermit, Jean paused. "You steer wrong," said the giant, speaking with an accent which at once reminded his hearer of that of the maiden; "your course is to the rising sun." "I go where I will," replied Jean, nettled at this unlooked-for interruption. "Youth," answered the other, "I have watched thee and wish thee well! rush not heedlessly to certain death!" "Stay me not!" resolutely answered Jean, wondering at the interest taken in him by this strange being. "Thou knowest not!" said the hermit sternly; "it is not only from death I wish to save thee, but from worse than death; I tell thee I—" He checked himself, as if fearful of saying too much, and bent his eyes searchingly into those of Jean, who murmured simply, "I am resolved." "Then God help thee and speed thee!" said the giant. Glancing into the boat he saw one of the curved and pierced shells then, as now, used by Guernsey seamen as signal-horns: pointing to it he said, "If in peril, where a blast may be heard on Lihou, sound the horn twice: it is a poor hope but may serve thee!" He was gone.

Jean paddled into the dreaded bay; the moon had now sunk and he was further favoured by a slight mist. Knowing the tides from infancy, he worked his way noiselessly till he approached where the Voizin fleet lay, then laid himself down and let the current take him.

He passed several boats in safety; as far as he could judge, from the observations he had taken from Lihou, he was nearly past the anchorage when a crash, succeeded by a grating sound, warned him of danger. A curse, followed by an ejaculation of surprise and pleasure, enlightened him as to the nature of the collision: he was in contact with one of the anchored vessels. "Odin is good!" cried a voice; "ha! a skiff drifted from a wrecked vessel! and all eyes but mine sleeping!" The speaker threw over a small anchor and grappled the boat. Jean was prepared; without a moment's hesitation he cut the anchor-rope: his craft drifted onwards, leaving the fisherman grumbling at the rottenness of his tackle. He offered a short prayer of gratitude, and in a few minutes ventured cautiously to resume his oars. He heard the breaking of the waves, but seamanship on the unknown and indistinct coast was useless. Two sharp blows, striking the boat in rapid succession, told him that he had touched a submerged rock; the strong tide carried him off it, but the water poured in through a gaping rent. He was now, however, on a sandy bottom: he sprang out, pulled the boat up as far as possible, and sat down to wait for light.

The first break of dawn showed him his position: he was facing northward; he was therefore on the Hanois arm of the bay. Fortune had indeed been kind to him, for he had drifted into a small cleft sheltered by precipitous rocks, a place where concealment was fairly possible, as it was accessible only by land at the lowest tides. He examined his store of provisions, which was uninjured; storing it among the rocks he rested till the sun sank. He then cautiously climbed the cliff, and looked on the scene revealed by the moonlight. Seawards stood a rough round tower; no other building was visible on the point, which seemed deserted. The loneliness gave him courage; when the moon set, the night being clear, he explored further and satisfied himself that there were no human beings, except the occupants of the tower, living on these rocks. He retired to his hiding-place to rest; before dawn he again ascended and concealed himself among the bracken and brambles which formed the only available shelter. During the whole day he saw but one person, an elderly woman, whose dark features and bright kerchief showed her to be of southern or gipsy origin, and who passed backwards and forwards carrying water to the tower. His examination increased his confidence; he calculated, by measuring the time occupied by the old woman in passing with an empty and returning with a full pitcher, that the spring frequented by her could not be far distant; at night he found it just beyond the junction of the rocks with the mainland. The water was cool and fresh, and considerably revived him; he noticed too that the luxuriant brushwood, nourished by the moisture, offered a good place for concealment; he returned, removed thither what remained of his provisions, and ensconced himself in his new retreat.

In the morning he saw two figures approaching from the tower; one was the same servant he had seen before, but the other!—his heart throbbed and leaped, his brain reeled, his eyes gazed hungrily; he could not be, he was not, mistaken!—the second figure was the heroine of his dreams! She walked silently. Jean saw that memory had not played him false: her beauty, her grace, were no freak of his imagination; would the holy father now say that she was a devil, while thus she moved in her loveliness, a woman to be loved and worshipped!—a very woman, too! not above the cares of life! Seating herself by the spring she despatched her companion on an errand to supply domestic wants, promising to await her return.

Jean's principal characteristic was rapid resolution: he reasoned that a small alarm might make the girl fly; that his chance of retaining her was an overpowering shock. He stepped boldly out and stood before her. The maiden sprang quickly to her feet; there was no terror in her face; she was of true blood; if she was afraid she did not show it; it was clear she recognized the apparition, but intense surprise, overpowering other emotions, kept her dumb. Jean had thus the chance of speaking first, and deftly he used his opportunity. In a few rapid sentences he told the tale of his search, of his adventures, of his selection of his hiding-place; then he paused. The maiden was not long in finding words. There was a flush on her cheek and a tear hanging on her eyelash which made Jean very happy. "You must go," she said, "but where? Your life is forfeit! forfeit to the Gods!" She shuddered as she said this. "In yonder tower lives my mother, on the shore are my people; there is no escape on either hand! A chance has saved you hitherto; none dare approach our home without my mother's permission, which is rarely given; but on this spot they may find you, may seize you, may—!" She stopped, with an expression of horror, and covered her face with her hands.

But Jean was not anxious; he was radiant with happiness. He seated himself and spoke of love, deep passionate love; so gentle was he, so soft, so courteous, and yet so ardent, that the maiden trembled; when he dared to take her hand she did not withdraw it. The moment of bliss was brief; a step was heard. "Hide yourself quickly," she whispered, "Tita is returning." Jean promptly obeyed the injunction. The old woman arrived with a well-filled wallet, and looked fondly at her young mistress. The signs of recent agitation struck her. "What has befallen thee, Hilda?" she cried anxiously. The girl took her arm and led her seawards. Jean, watching, could see the start and angry expression of the older, the coaxing, pleading attitude of the younger woman; he could satisfy himself that the resistance of the former was gradually being overcome, and as they returned he saw that the maiden's victory was indisputable. She summoned Jean, who was inspected by Tita at first with distrust, then with modified approval. "You must stay here," said the maiden earnestly, "closely hidden till nightfall; my absence has been already sufficiently long, and nothing can be done while daylight lasts." Bidding him farewell she sped with her guardian towards the tower, while Jean retired to his bushes a prey to fond thoughts and feverish hopes.

Before sundown he saw the tall figure of the sorceress wending landwards. She did not approach the spring. Hilda quickly followed with her former companion. "We have a long journey," she said, "and short time: we must start at once." Removing all traces of his lair he obeyed without hesitation. They ascended the steep cliff. The night was clear, the moon at this hour was bright and lustrous. "We have three hours," said the maiden, "ere we leave our guest!"—she looked archly at Jean as she thus described him—"it should suffice!" They were now on the heights of Pleinmont; no one was moving, though voices of men and beasts could be plainly heard in the distance. "They feast to-night to the Gods," said Hilda; "we need fear only some belated laggard!" The heather was not yet springing, but Jean could see that gorse was on the bloom, which he considered a favourable omen: they stepped out bravely on the short springy turf. Tita's steps were slower than those of the young pair, who were deaf to her calls for delay. Never to his dying day did Jean forget that happy night-walk. His soul was poured out in love, and he knew that his love was returned. He was steeped to the full in joy; no thought of future cares or perils crossed his mind. They had passed three or four headlands before the girl halted and waited for her attendant, who came up muttering to herself and grumbling; compliments from Jean and caresses from Hilda restored her good humour, and the work of the evening commenced. "Follow me closely," said the girl; "let your eye be keen and your step firm: the descent is no child's sport." Jean looked at the cliff, fitted for the flight of gull or cormorant rather than the foot of man, still less of gentle maiden: Hilda was already over the brink: Jean, following, saw that she was on a path no broader than a goat's track; the difficulties of the descent need not be described; it was possible for a clear head and practised foot, to the nervous or the unsteady the attempt must have been fatal. Arrived at the bottom the climbers found themselves in a small cleft strewn with huge boulders; the rocks towered high above them. Hilda glanced at the moon. "We must be quick," said she, showing him some deep caverns in the rock; "there," she said, "is your home. Here you are safe; my mother alone knows the secret of these caves. I must mount again; you must climb with me to mark the path more closely." She sprang to the rock and commenced to ascend as nimbly as she had come down. Jean saw the necessity of taking every precaution; he noted carefully each feature of the track. Arrived at the summit she bade him farewell. She pointed out a place where Tita would from time to time leave him provisions, and said that he would find water in the caves; she then tripped quickly off. Jean did not linger, seeing that if he did so light would fail him for his return. He crossed the track for the third time, reached the caves, and slept soundly till dawn.

When he awoke he inspected his strange retreat. He was in a large hall, two hundred feet long, and some fifty feet high and broad; this chamber was entered by a small orifice of no great length, through which he had passed on the preceding night; it was warm, and dry except where the stream of which Hilda had spoken trickled through to the sea. It was the fissure now known as the Creux Mahie, and to which an easy access has been arranged for the benefit of the curious. Here Jean passed three months. Hilda frequently visited

21

him, and always kept him supplied with food; she warned him also when he might safely roam on the cliffs above. There was no obstacle to her visits, even when they extended to a considerable length, as the mother seemed always to be satisfied as to her absences when Tita accompanied her; and the latter, whose infirmities prevented her from descending, had no means of shortening the interviews.

Thus the lovers had opportunity to study each other's characters. The maiden's pure heart knew no distrust, and Jean was faithful and chivalrous as Sir Galahad. They spoke not always of love: words were unnecessary to explain what every look betokened. Jean found her skilled in strange, mystical, lore, but ignorant of all that sways and rules mankind. The history of the selfish struggles of human interests and passions was to her a sealed book. She had been carefully shrouded from the knowledge of evil; but, in order to protect her in the rough turbulent little world in which she lived, it had been necessary to keep her from association with her countrymen, and so she had never mingled with them except under the charge of her mother, in whose presence the fiercest were submissive. Jean, therefore, in speaking to her of family intercourse, of the intermingling of members of the household, of bright chat with friends, opened up to her views of life of which she had formed no conception. Then he told her of his own people; described the three generations living under one roof; depicted the daily round, the care of the old and the young, the work, the return of the workers to their wives, sisters, and children, the love of the mothers for their infants, the reverence for age, the strong mutual affection of husband and wife, brother and sister. To these descriptions she listened with a happy smile, the mission of woman dawning on her; and many were the questions she asked, till she seemed to have mastered the pictures painted for her. Above all, Jean strained to bring her to the knowledge of the God of the Christian, for he himself was an earnest, intelligent disciple. He found her mind clearer than he had expected. Judith (this he now knew was the mother's name) was a remarkable woman; her mind was lofty, if darkened. While others were satisfied with the grossness of a material creed her spirit soared aloft. Her Gods commanded her implicit faith, her unswerving allegiance. Seated on the storm-clouds, sweeping through space, they represented to her infinite force. She attributed to them no love for mankind, which was in her creed rather their plaything, but she credited them with the will and the power to scatter good and ill before they claimed the soul of the hero to their fellowship, or cast into a lower abyss that of the coward or the traitor. She believed that she saw their giant forms half bending from their vapoury thrones, and she thought that she read their decrees. Sorceress she may have been; in those days sorcery was attributed to many who had obtained a knowledge of laws of nature, then considered occult, now recognized among the guiding principles from which scientific deductions are drawn. She believed in the power of magic, which she was universally understood to possess; but she was no vulgar witch: rather was she a worthy priestess of her not ignoble deities. The effect upon Hilda's mind of the teachings of such a woman is easy to conceive. She had been allowed to know little of the wild orgies of the barbaric feasts offered to the Gods by her countrymen, of their brutal excesses, of their human sacrifices: from this knowledge she had been as far as possible shielded: she knew only of the dim mystic beings, half men, half Gods, from whose wrath she shrank with terror. To a mind so constituted and trained the revelation of the story of the infant Christ was a passionate pleasure. She never tired of listening to the tale of the birth in the stable of Bethlehem; but she loved not to dwell on the history of the passion and death, which was at that time beyond her understanding. She drank in with parted lips all that concerned the Holy Mother, of whom she was never weary of hearing. Jean had a rude drawing of the Madonna and Child, given him by Father Austin: the figures had the angularity and rigidity of Byzantine art, but the artist had represented his subject with reverence, and no lack of skill, and she loved to dwell on the pure mother's face, and on the longing look in the eyes of the Child. She accepted wholly the idea of a God who loved mankind, of infinite goodness and mercy: if she could not as yet enter into the subtlety of doctrine she could give that childlike faith which is the envy of doctrinarians.

CHAPTER IV.

REVELATION.

"I curse the hand that did the deid,
The heart that thocht the ill,
The feet that bore him wi' sik speid,
The comely youth to kill."

*Gil Morrice.* —OLD BALLAD.

Jean had often expressed his curiosity to see the interior of the tower, and Hilda had promised to gratify it. On the 25th of October an opportunity occurred. She informed her lover that on that day a feast of unusual importance would be held from which none would be absent, and that her mother would be engaged at it from noon to midnight. On that day, therefore, he walked freely along the cliffs, and was admitted to the dwelling. He had unconsciously based his idea of its contents upon his recollections of the squalid abode of Marie Torode, where human skulls, skeletons, bones of birds and beasts, dried skins, and other ghastly objects had been so grouped as to add to the superstitious feeling inspired by the repulsive appearance of the crone herself. His astonishment was therefore proportionate when he saw what to his eyes appeared exceptional luxury. A wooden partition divided the room on the lower story into two chambers of unequal size: the larger, in which he stood, was the common dwelling apartment, the other was given over to Hilda. The upper story, approached by a ladder and also by an external staircase, was sacred to Judith; Tita occupied some outbuildings. The sitting-room was hung with rich stuffs of warm and glowing colours; here and there fitful rays of the sun flickered upon gold brocade and Oriental embroidery; rugs and mats, which must have been offered for sale in the bazaars of Egypt and Morocco, were littered about in strange contrast with the bracken-strewed floor. On the walls were inlaid breastplates and helmets, pieces of chain armour, swords and daggers of exquisite workmanship. On shelves stood drinking vessels of rougher make, but the best that northern craftsmen could produce. The seats were rude and massive: one of them, placed by a window fronting the setting sun, was evidently the favourite resting-place of Judith. Above this seat was a shelf on which lay some of the mysterious scrolls of which Jean had seen specimens in the possession of the fathers. Instruments of witchcraft, if such existed, must have been in the upper story: none were visible. All this splendour was manifestly inconsistent with the homely taste and abstracted mode of thought of the sorceress. In point of fact she was hardly aware of its existence. The decorator was Tita, in whom was the instinct of the connoisseur, supported by no inconsiderable knowledge to which she had attained in those early years of which she never could be induced to speak. When a rich prize was brought into the bay, freighted with a cargo from Asia, Africa, or the European shores of the Mediterranean, she never failed to attend the unloading, during which, by the help of cajolery, judicious depreciation, and other ingenious devices still dear to the virtuoso, she succeeded in obtaining possession of articles which would have enraptured a modern collector. Judith was apparently indifferent to a habit which she looked upon as a caprice of her faithful servant, and the only evidence of her noticing it was her concentration in her own apartments of all that related to her personal studies and pursuits.

It was now Jean's turn to listen and learn, and Hilda's to explain and instruct. Towards nine o'clock he was preparing to return. He was indifferent to the darkness, as by this time he knew the track so well that he crossed it fearlessly at all hours. His hand was on the bolt when Tita announced in alarm that Judith was returning and was on the point of entering. Hardly was there time to conceal him behind the hangings before she appeared. Her countenance was pale and worn, her tone, as Hilda took off her outer garments was weary and sad. "The portents were hostile and dangerous," she said; "they foretold woe, disaster, ruin. Will the mighty ones reveal to me the future? I cannot tell! But my spirit must commune with them till dawn breaks. Dost hear them? They call me now!" She held up her finger as a sudden blast rocked the tower to its foundations. "Aye," she continued more firmly after a pause, "they will not forget those who are true to them. But this people! this people!" She hid her face with her hands as if to cover a painful vision. After a time she rose to her feet and took the girl by the hand. Leading her to the seat by the window on which she placed herself, and making her kneel by her side, she said—

"Hilda! the chill mist closes round! my life draws to its end! Nay, weep not, child! were it not for thee I would long ere this have prayed the gods my masters to remove me from my sojourn among the degenerate sons of our noble fathers; but I trembled for thy fate, sweet one!" These last words were almost inexpressibly tender. "I dared not trust thy slight frame to battle unsheltered with the storm. Now the blast summoning me is sounded. I cannot much longer disobey, though I may crave for brief respite. But I have found thee refuge! thou wilt be in a safe haven. Stay! I must speak while the spirit is on me!"

Roquaine Bay with l'Erée and Lihou. Sketched in 1887.

"Mother!" sobbed the girl, clasping the old woman's knees.

"Hilda!" said Judith slowly, "call me no longer by that name! I am not thy mother; before men only do I call thee daughter. Silence!" she exclaimed imperatively, as Hilda looked quickly up, doubting whether she heard aright. "Silence! and listen!"

"I have loved thee truly, child, and have nurtured thee as a mother would! and thou art no stranger! the same blood runs in our veins! Yes! thou art mine! for thy father was my brother. Does not that give thee to me? Hush! thou shalt hear the tale."

Hilda's were not the only ears that drank in every word of the following story.

"Twenty years ago what a demi-god was Haco! He was a giant, but even men who feared him loved him. Though brave and strong as Odin himself, his mind was gentle and kind as a maiden's; first in council, in war, in manly sports, he ever had an open ear and a helping hand for the troubled and distressed. He was adored, nay, worshipped, by all. What wonder then that when he and the proud chief Algar courted the same maiden, he was preferred! Thou knowest not, Hilda, the mysteries of a tender heart; may it be long indeed before thy heart is seared by human passion!" It was fortunate that darkness hid the burning blush which suffused Hilda's face and neck at this pious wish. Judith proceeded:—"Thy father wedded and thou wast born. He poured on thy infant form all the wealth of his great generous heart. Algar nursed his revenge: he dared not act openly, for our house was as noble as his own—nay, nobler!" she added haughtily, "but he bided his time. Haco's tower was near the shore, a pleasant, lovely, spot. One night the news was borne to me that enemies had landed, and that his dwelling was in flames; I hurried towards it; I was stopped by armed warriors; Algar's men, they said, had hastened to the rescue; the chief had ordered that no women should leave their homes. It was in vain that I urged and protested. When at last I reached the spot the struggle was said to be over, and the assailants, beaten off, were declared to have sailed away. Algar himself came to me with well-assumed grief. He had arrived, he swore, too late to save. The tower had been fired whilst the inmates slept, the wife and child had perished; Haco, after performing incredible feats of valour, had fallen before the strokes of numerous foes; when he himself had come with a chosen band, while sending the rest of his forces to other posts which the unforeseen danger might threaten, nothing remained but to avenge the murder. Why recount the caitiffs lies? Where were the signs of landing, of hasty re-embarkation? Where were the dead of the strangers? Thrown into the sea! he said; it was foul falsehood, and fouler treachery. I found your father's body; he was smitten and gashed, but nobler than the living. I touched him and was silent. I knew what none others guessed. I arose. The spirits of the Gods came over me, and I cursed his slayer. Never had I spoken so fiercely; men stood and wondered. I prayed the Gods to make the wretch who had caused my darling's death miserable by land and by sea, by day and by night, in the field and at the board, loathed by his friends, and scorned by his foes. The Gods heard my imprecations; as I turned my eyes skywards they looked from their clouds, wrath kindling on their brows, and Algar's face was white with fear, his hand trembled and his knee shook.

"'We must bury him,' he faltered.

"'Yea,' said I, 'but in a hero's grave, and after the custom of our fathers.'

"There was a murmur of applause. Algar could not refuse.

"They brought the choicest of the boats, they made the sails bright and gay, they put in it the dead man's arms, and food to accompany him to the land of spirits. Then they bound him before the mast, his face turned seaward. At sundown they towed the boat to deep water, so pierced her that she might sink slowly under the waves, and then they left the hero to his rest. I had gone out with them: alone I said to him my last farewell. But they did not know my secret. They did not guess that I had ascertained by my art that life was yet in him, that I had poured between his lips subtle drops which would maintain animation for many days and nights, during which consciousness might be restored; nor did they imagine that when I kneeled before him I had stopped the leak by which the water was to flow into the doomed boat. Algar was now the deceived; it was a living man, not a corpse, who started on that voyage. Haco lives still, though where my art cannot tell. I thought that Marie Torode knew, and sought her on her death-bed to question her, but either she could not or she would not tell." Hilda's mind was in such confusion that she could not speak. The old woman continued. "Algar lived on—yes, lived that he might suffer all the evils with which my curse loaded him, and died that he might be hurled into the abyss where traitors and cravens writhe and groan. Enough of him!

"When I returned to my tower, a figure was crouching before the hearth: it was Tita, and you were in her arms. The faithful creature, whom your father had chosen from a band of captives to be your nurse, had, unperceived, saved your life from the flames. Thenceforward you were my care. I took your mother's place as best I could. Others knew not your parentage, nor did they dare to question me. None suspected the truth."

When she reached this point she bent over the kneeling girl and gave her a kiss, tender as a mother's if not a mother's kiss; her fingers caressed the head bowed upon her knees; for a time the silence was only broken by Hilda's sobs. She then spoke again, this time quickly, sternly, as if to prevent interruption.

"I cannot leave thee alone, and I will not! Listen, child, and be silent! What I now tell thee is beyond thy young understanding: thou hast but to shape thy will to my bidding: it is for me to launch thy vessel on its voyage, the Gods will help thy riper judgment to steer its course! The time has come when thou must wed! I have chosen for thee a suitor, the chief to whom all thy countrymen bend the knee. Garthmund claims thee as his bride; ere eight days expire the marriage feast will be held. He is of noble birth, there is none nobler; he is young and strong, and should be favoured by the Gods if he prove worthy of them. He is a fitting bridegroom for Haco's daughter."

The girl was dazed and trembling. She knew this chief: he answered Judith's description, but was rough and coarse. Had she not met Jean she might not have dared to refuse, but now she felt that death would be more welcome than this marriage. "Spare me, mother!" she said, as if she had not heard the disclaimer of maternity. "I am too young, too weak." The old woman pressed her hand on the girl's lips. "We will not speak further to-night," she said; "thou canst not see Garthmund for three days, for so long the feast will last. May the Gods protect thee!" She rose: the fitful moonlight streamed on her gaunt form; she turned and slowly ascended to her chamber.

The terrified girl quickly released Jean, who led her from the tower. If she was broken and trembling he was erect and resolute; no longer the soft lover, but the prompt man of action. She felt the bracing influence. "We have three days," he said. "Within that time we must flee. I will not return to the cave; my task must be to repair the boat."

He mentioned certain articles which he begged her to provide, pressed her to his breast, and disappeared in the darkness.

At daylight he examined the little vessel. She was no worse than she had been, as each incoming tide, reaching the place where she was secured, had floated her, but the rock had opened a large jagged fissure. Hilda brought him such materials as she could procure, a log of wood, bark which she stitched with her own hands, a hatchet and nails. Jean utilized also the vraick with which the sand was strewn. He worked without fear of detection, knowing that the whole population was inland; but the lovers had to rely on themselves alone, for, when there was a question of flight, Tita was no longer to be trusted.

On the third day Jean found the boat fairly seaworthy. Hilda felt a severe pang at leaving Judith, who had not reverted to the subject of her marriage. Whether her parent or not, she loved her dearly; she felt also the pain of parting with Tita, but her resolution never swerved. She had given her heart to Jean; she felt also a presentiment that she would discover her father; while it was her belief that the parting from her old associates was but temporary.

When the sun went down Jean set his sail, meaning to make a rapid dash across the bay, and seeing no cause for concealing his movements. There was more swell than he liked for so frail a craft, but wind and tide were favourable to the enterprise, and the night was exceptionally bright, the moon being full; this brightness would have been fatal had the inhabitants been on the alert, but under present circumstances the pale beams were welcome. Hilda took the helm; she knew every passage in the labyrinth of submerged rocks, and they were soon in comparatively open water. Jean then assumed control, wrapping the maiden in his cloak, for the waves were tossing their spray over the boat as she heeled over to the breeze.

They had traversed in safety three-fourths of their course when Jean, looking seaward, saw a dark sail bearing down on them. One of the pirate ships, delayed by contrary winds, was hurrying homeward, the crew of five men hoping to arrive ere the feast was over. Jean's hope that the boat might not be discovered was soon dispelled: the vessel altered her course slightly and hailed. Jean made no answer.

The pirate was evidently in no mood to parley; the crew were in a fierce temper, angry and discontented at the postponement of their arrival. She made a deliberate attempt to run the boat down. Jean divined her object and, putting up his helm sharply at the right moment, let her shoot by him astern; he then resumed his course. A second attempt was clumsier, and was easily evaded; the assailants were hurried and impatient; nor did they know the seamanlike qualities of the man with whom they were dealing. But Jean saw that ultimate escape was hopeless, and this was equally apparent to Hilda who, however, though pale as death, gave a firm pressure of the hand in response to his grasp. At this moment an object glimmered under the youth's feet: stooping down he touched the shell. The hermit's parting words flashed on his mind: he seized on the hope of rescue, and sounded two loud and clear blasts.

The pirates now altered their tactics. Handling their vessel with more care they succeeded, after two or three unsuccessful attempts, in ranging alongside and grappling the boat. A man sprung on board and seized Hilda. "A rare booty!" he cried, —"the Gods repent of their waywardness." Jean was engaged with those of the crew who had seized the boat; the man laughingly gave the girl a rough embrace: it was the last act he had to record before entering the spirit world. Hilda drew from her bosom one of the daggers which Jean had noticed on the tower walls, whose blade, still sharp and keen, might have been forged by a Damascus smith; it struck deep to the heart of the ruffian, who fell lifeless into the waves. Jean had now freed the craft, but the respite was short: before she had made much progress she was again captured. The pirates, furious at the death of their comrade, made a determined onslaught. Jean, fighting desperately, received from behind a terrific blow which laid him senseless. But a superstitious feeling made them hesitate before committing further outrage; they had recognized Hilda, and feared the consequence of Judith's vengeance if she were injured. There was no time, however, for delay; the, rude repairs, torn by the trampling feet, had given way, and the leak had re-opened: the boat was fast sinking. The pirates cared not for Jean's lifeless body; that might sink or swim; but they felt they must save the girl whatever might be her future doom. Even their hearts softened somewhat as they watched her erect in the sinking boat, her face pallid, her fair hair shining in the moonlight, but her lips set, her lovely eyes bent tearless on her prostrate lover, her right hand, holding the blood-stained dagger, hanging listlessly by her side.

Watching an opportunity, a stalwart youth seized her from behind and pinned her arms. The next moment he himself was seized as if he were a dog, and hurled into the water. The new combatant, whose arrival had so effectually changed the aspect of affairs, was the hermit, who followed up his first stroke by another still more decisive. Springing into the pirate craft, wrenching a weapon from the grasp of the chief of the assailants, he drove before him the three remaining men, terror-struck at his sudden and inexplicable appearance, his superhuman size and strength. One by one he swept them overboard; then grasping a huge stone, which formed part of the ballast, he dashed it with the full force of his gigantic strength through the planks of the boat, which at once began to fill. All this was the work of a few moments. He then leaped into the skiff, which sank as he swiftly transferred to his own vessel its two occupants.

Before another hour was over, Jean, stretched on a pallet, was receiving the attention of loving hands in a cell of the Lihou monastery.

## CHAPTER V.

## AFFLICTION.

"The race of Thor and Odin
Held their battles by my side,
And the blood of man was mingling
Warmly with my chilly tide."

*Danube and the Euxine.* —AYTOUN.

Father Austin received his pupil's companion with the courtesy due
to her distress, but with much misgiving. After tending his patient,
whose situation was critical, he paced thoughtfully towards the cell
in which he had placed her, revolving in his mind the difficulties of
the case. His amazement was intense when he slowly opened the
door. The maiden was kneeling, her back towards him; before her
was the little picture of the Madonna; she was praying aloud; her
words were simple but passionately pathetic; she threw herself and
her lover upon the mercy of the Holy Mother with a trust so
absolute, a confidence so infinite, that the monk could hardly refrain
from tears. How had he been blinded! as he looked and listened the
scales fell from his eyes: he humbly owned his error.

The noise of his step startled her; she rose and looked at him
inquiringly. "Maiden," he said, answering her appealing look, "his
fate is in the hands of God, whose ears are ever open to the prayers
of those that fear Him."

Often and often had Jean spoken to her of Father Austin; she loved
him already, but she had yet to fathom the nobleness of his soul. His
single-heartedness and abnegation of self, his tenderness and quick
sympathy (virtues tempering his fierce abhorrence of Paganism), his
stern reprobation of the evil, and his yearning for the good, in the
untutored barbarians among whom he laboured, were gradually
revealed in the discourses which they held daily while Jean lay
between life and death. Reaping and garnering what Jean had sown,
he scattered fresh seed, opening out to her the great history of God
in man. Qualities hitherto unsuspected in her developed; if an apt

pupil, she was an instructive teacher of the wealth of charity and purity that dwells in an untainted woman's heart. And she had another friend: the hermit watched over her with touching care and assiduity. He appeared strangely attracted to her; the holy fathers marvelled to see this rough being, who had seemed to them an animal to be feared while pitied, caring for the maiden's comfort with a woman's gentleness: he seemed never weary of contemplating her, sometimes murmuring to himself as he did so. Any little delicacy that the island could afford, game, fish, shellfish, was provided for her by him. Once, thinking her couch hard, he disappeared and returned bearing, whence none knew, soft stuffs better fitted for her tender form; on this occasion the whole man seemed transformed, when he stepped in with a smile in his big frank eyes, and a ruddy glow on his bronzed scarred cheeks, placed his offering at her feet, and strode away. Strange, too, to say, Hilda seemed to return the feeling: happy in the presence of Austin, she was yet with him as the pupil with the master; but with the recluse she was gentle, affectionate, and even playful. The monks attempted not to solve the puzzle of the bond that knitted together the two strange beings; analysis of character troubled little their saintly minds.

At length consciousness returned; Jean opened his eyes and recognised Austin. This was a joyful moment. Quiet was all that was now necessary to complete the restoration of his health, which could not, however, be anticipated for a considerable time. The first inquiry of the patient was for Hilda, and he was allowed to see her; on the next day they were permitted to interchange a few words, after which Austin explained what he had already decided. Hilda, he pointed out, could not fitly remain in Lihou, where she had been allowed to reside only until her lover was out of danger; the laws of the establishment, which forbade the presence of women, must now be put in force, but a fitting home had been provided for her; she would be placed with the Sisters at the Vale; the hermit would conduct her thither on the following day. The girl bowed to this decision, sorely as she grieved to leave him she loved; the next morning they parted, and she embarked with her guardian who, shielding her lovingly from all harm, placed her, ere nightfall, in her new abode.

Judith had not discovered the girl's departure till the sun was well up, when she heard of her absence from the frantic Tita. The old woman's force of character was colossal; pettinesses, small passions, were unknown to her. Had her sphere been larger her promptitude of resource, keenness of perception, resolute look onwards and upwards, solidity of purpose, and incisive action might have graven her name on the tables of history. Stagnating in the shallow pools of the unstoried rocks in which she passed her life, these grand qualities were wasted and perverted. She lost no time now in recrimination; a few sharp questions enabled her to judge how far the weakness of affection had played the traitor with the old woman, whom she left to settle matters with her own conscience. She saw Garthmund, and told him that, in consequence of the unsatisfactory augury of the last sacrifice, she had decided to postpone the marriage. Nor did she appear to notice the indifference with which the chief, who could not pretend that he ardently loved a bride who was practically a stranger to him, received the decision. It took her some time to discover where Hilda had taken refuge; it speaks ill for female reticence that she discovered it shortly after the girl's removal to the sisterhood. She satisfied herself that her own people had no suspicion of the flight, as none of the crew of the belated boat had reached the shore; and she gathered, from the transfer of the maiden to the convent, that Father Austin was, on his side, resolved not to make known the elopement of Garthmund's intended wife. Her paramount wish was to recover her niece, but she perceived that she must act warily, and must be ready to deal with the many contingencies which would inevitably arise during the development of her schemes. Hilda's position under the immediate protection of the religious communities was a serious obstacle. Judith believed that against them her magic arts would be of no avail; she was therefore driven to confine herself to earthly combinations; but she was in no wise daunted by this difficulty, which in point of fact cleared her judgment, and assisted her by inducing her to make the best of the materials at her disposal. The obvious plan for the recovery of the girl was to induce Garthmund to attack the nunnery, and drag his bride from it; but to this there were many objections. Acknowledgment of Hilda's flight would be in itself a confession of failure. She had promised to produce the girl when she was required; to seek the chief's assistance to enable her to fulfil the promise would be a diminution of her prestige, and consequently of her power. Again, it was by no means certain that the chief who, it has been said, was no love-sick bridegroom, would consent to undertake the enterprise; nor, if he did undertake it, was his prospect of success unquestionable, for the islanders, though not ready listeners to the Christian teaching, would have united to repel a heathen attack on their teachers whom they honoured and respected. Judith therefore rejected this expedient, arranging her plan of operations with remarkable ingenuity.

Her first aim was to promote ill-feeling between the Voizins and their neighbours; this part of the campaign was prosecuted with vigour. Cattle were lost on either side of the boundary; houses were burnt; old wells ran dry; rumours, mysteriously circulated, spoke of these as no accidental mishaps; suspicions were whispered; instances of retaliation followed. At the time when a dangerous feeling was thus growing up a famine broke out in the Voizin country while the islanders were well supplied. The hungry Voizin men heard voices in the darkness scoffing at them, laughter and sneers. When their carts were sent to fetch the necessaries of life, lynch-pins were loosened; in more than one case the draught oxen were houghed; the provisions, when received, were mouldy and unwholesome. At last sickness broke out, with stories of poison; then the tension became insupportable. The Voizin chief, too proud to go to his neighbours, summoned them to him; the messenger was murdered. This assassination, of which the natives denied all knowledge, was met by prompt reprisals; three Perelle fishermen were hung on the spot where the body was found. From this date the outbreak of hostilities was but a question of time. A sternness of purpose ruled in the councils of the Voizins which frustrated all attempts at conciliation. A little before Christmas a trivial incident kindled the smouldering flames, and the hordes, pouring from the Torteval valleys, swept over the districts now known as the parishes of St. Saviour's and the Câtel; the resistance was tame and ineffectual, sufficient only to give occasion for considerable slaughter and plunder. The invaders, seeing no reason for returning to their famine-stricken fastnesses, settled themselves in the enjoyment of the abundance of the vanquished, who, in their turn, with their accustomed versatility, submitted patiently, and even cheerfully, to a yoke which, after the first onslaught was over, pressed lightly; the Voizins, to whom fighting was a pastime, bearing no malice, and passing imperceptibly into a genial mood.

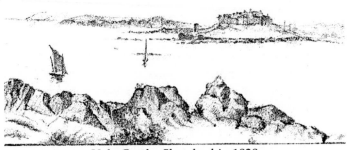

Vale Castle. Sketched in 1838

Judith now prepared to develop the next move, the object of which was to undermine the authority of the monks, and make them vulnerable by isolation. Derisive hints were dropped respecting the failure of the new religion to help its votaries in the hour of peril; the victory of the Voizins was attributed to the superiority of their Gods rather than to deficiency in courage on the part of their foes: this theory, which was not unpalatable to those who had been half-hearted in defence of their homes, was also utilized by the more sober spirits as an argument wherewith to restrain the more ardent from attempting to renew the struggle under similar conditions. The observances of the religion of Thor and Odin, or rather of that debased form of it which prevailed among this singular people, were celebrated under their more alluring aspects: frequent feasts and dances captivated the laughter-loving islanders, who had been tried somewhat severely by the severity of the *régime* which Austin had endeavoured to impose since he had seen danger in his damaging encounter with Judith. After a time it was proclaimed that none would be permitted to join in the revelries who were enemies to the Gods who presided at them. This stroke was successful: the majority openly embraced the creed of their conquerors, and showed the usual spirit of perverts in exceeding the latter in their zeal to sweep away all traces of the religion which they had abandoned. The minority who held true to their faith drew together, a grim and resolute band, prepared for a bold defence and, if Christ so willed it, for martyrdom.

It was not Judith's purpose, now that the disruption of the islanders was effected, to leave time for the Christians to mature plans for resistance. Garthmund, at her instigation, delivered simultaneous attacks on Lihou and the Vale; he himself superintending the latter operation in order that he might see that the sorceress's instructions, that all in the nunnery were to be made prisoners uninjured, and brought to her closely veiled, were implicitly obeyed. To the surprise of the islanders, however, both assaults, though made with spirit and absolute confidence of success, were completely repulsed; the same result attended a renewed attack, made two days subsequently with fresh and increased forces supported by native levies. Garthmund found that in both places he had before him not only resolute troops, but skilled and enterprising commanders.

## CHAPTER VI.

## CONSOLATION.

"Mother! list a suppliant child!
Ave Maria!
Ave Maria! Stainless styled.
Foul demons of the earth and air,
From this their wonted haunt exiled,
Shall flee before thy presence fair."

*Lady of the Lake.* — WALTER SCOTT.

Jean's recovery after Hilda's departure had been slow and lingering; but for the unwearied care of the good fathers and of the recluse, aided by a constitution of no ordinary strength, he must have succumbed to the terrible injuries which he had received. As, however, the days began to lengthen, and signs of spring to appear even on the wild rock where he had taken refuge, his vigour gradually returned. It had been necessary that he should be protected from excitement; consequently, while receiving from the hermit regular reports from the Vale, and many a sweet message from his love which made his heart leap with happiness, he knew nothing till the beginning of February of the incursion of the Voizins, and the accompanying events. Since he had been alone, however, he had dwelt for hours together on the strange story which he had overheard in the tower, the principal figure of which, while his brain had been still confused, had been always mingled in his delirium with the massive form of the hermit. Father Austin, watching him with anxiety, at length suggested that he should relieve his mind by repeating the tale to the recluse himself. He readily adopted the suggestion. His listener, who had been too delicate to question Hilda as to her antecedents, but who had been burning to learn the explanation of the striking resemblance of her features to a face which, whether he waked or slept, ever haunted him, though more often contorted in agony than wreathed in smiles, heard with impatience the history of Algar's treachery; but when Jean detailed the escape of Tita and her charge, and identified the latter with the maiden whom he had rescued, he sprang to his feet at the risk of plunging his patient into a fresh crisis of fever, and exclaimed, "May the choicest gifts of heaven be showered on thee, brave youth! the blessed angels and saints will love thee for this deed!" He reflected a moment, then turned his eyes full on Jean's face, "Why should I leave it to Austin to tell thee what he has long known under the solemn secrecy which binds priest and sinner? Thou shalt know it from my own lips: I am Haco! Drifted hitherward on that lonely voyage, I was released by holy men, now saints above, who healed my wounds and taught me to bury my pride, and to kneel humbly before the Cross. I never doubted that I was childless as well as wifeless; had I done so, I should have returned at all risks to claim my own. But she! Hilda! 'twas her mother's name! this maiden, towards whom my soul went out in yearning, is my own! yes! my child! If a wild feeling rose when I watched her I crushed it out, for I thought that I had stifled all human passions; but now —" He fell on his knees, and hid his face in his hands, his giant frame convulsed with sobs; but it was evident that he was controlling himself, and when he rose his rugged face was full of humanity: youth seemed to have returned to it; under the disfiguring scars Jean could trace without difficulty the fearless, generous features of which Judith had spoken with such enthusiasm. Haco warmly grasped the sick man's hand, and left the cell.

Father Austin had, it appeared, learnt Judith's story from Hilda, but this confidence also had been made under the seal of confession. He had been confirmed in his impression of its accuracy by the tale he had already heard from Haco, whose strange arrival was still a favourite topic among the monks, though none of those now in the monastery had witnessed it. The three men were now able openly to discuss the subject in its various bearings, but they agreed that the mystery should not be revealed till peace was restored.

Haco had from the first foreseen the danger to be apprehended from the Voizin incursion. The monks were still further surprised to see the being, whose gentleness had amazed them on Hilda's arrival, now a leader of men, active, vigorous, inspiring others with the love of life with which he himself seemed to be animated. Before the attack came Jean was sufficiently recovered to be able to render efficient assistance; he had ably seconded Haco in the two encounters, after which he was specially entrusted with the defence of the Vale.

Judith was in no degree daunted by temporary failure: her nature revelled in overcoming opposition; her spirit rose to the occasion. Garthmund was inclined to be sulky after his second defeat, and might have abandoned the enterprise had he dared to do so; but fear of the sorceress kept him firm. For a month the system of blockade was tried, varied by occasional assaults which, being made with less spirit than the earlier ones, were easily repulsed. The blockade was not more successful. Haco had provided ample stores for the small garrison which he had considered sufficient to protect the promontory of Lihou, naturally almost impregnable; and the force defending the Vale, camped chiefly on Lancresse Common, was only nominally blockaded. The sallies, made from time to time, were ordered more with a view of keeping up the martial spirit of the men than with that of providing for wants, for the friendly inhabitants of the eastern side of the island, emboldened by recent proofs that the dreaded Voizins were not invincible, ran their boats almost with impunity into the little creeks into which the heavier craft of the enemy could not follow them.

Judith hardly noticed these details. Her attention was fixed upon the key of the position. She knew that a resistance of this description was altogether contrary to the unwarlike character of the natives; she was convinced that they were actuated by some abnormal spirit, and that if the motive power were removed the machine would collapse. She made it her business to ascertain what the spring was that guided them. All her art failed in detecting the presence of Haco, perhaps because her engines were powerless when directed against one of her own blood; but she easily ascertained that the warriors in the opposing camp looked to Jean as their leader, that his spirit pervaded all, and that his ardour to protect his sacred charge filled him with a wondrous power which astonished even those who from childhood had bent to his unchallenged primacy.

Having satisfied herself as to the character of the opposing force, her next step was to secure Jean's person. This presented no difficulty to her. A scroll was delivered to the young leader by an unknown messenger, who at once disappeared. Jean, seeing that the characters were those which, as he believed, Austin alone was able to trace, took the scroll to the sister who alone was able to interpret them. What Sister Theresa read was alarming:—"Hasten! I am grievously sick; my strength fails! I must see thee without delay." Jean was distressed beyond measure, but Hilda, whom he hurried to consult, agreed with him that no time must be lost in obeying the summons; the fact that Haco was at Lihou convinced them that the father would not have sent for Jean if his case had not been one of extreme danger. After a hasty farewell and a promise of speedy return, for his presence with the forces was imperative and he grudged every hour of absence from his beloved, he set out alone in his boat. Before an hour had passed he was captured by a flotilla which had been lying in ambuscade behind the Grandes Rocques, and was a prisoner in the enemy's camp.

If Judith had been an ordinary woman she would have been content with this result, would have executed the prisoner, and have awaited the submission of his disheartened followers; and she would have failed, defeated by the indomitable courage and resource of Haco. But it was not in this clumsy fashion that her genius moulded the materials at her command. She now controlled, as she believed, the mainspring of the resistance, which would probably cease with the death of Jean. But her aim went far beyond the mere submission of her antagonists; she wished that the blow should be struck in such a manner as to stamp out the false creed which had held the islanders in thrall, to prove to all sceptics the powers of her own Gods and the impotence of those of her opponents, and to commit the recently reconverted islanders so irretrievably that they could not afterwards backslide. She wished also, by making an example that would inspire terror, to establish the undisputed supremacy of her people in the whole island. But, side by side with these political considerations, were the religious influences honestly and steadfastly working in her powerful intellect. When she communed with her Gods she thought of no earthly good or ill: she loved these strange conceptions, and fixed her whole soul on conciliating them. It was now her conviction that they were displeased: their displeasure, awful as she believed it to be, did not terrify her, but it vexed her to the inmost heart: she feared that they had not been rightly propitiated, and resolved that the shortcoming must be remedied.

All her reflections pointed with unerring force to the same conclusion. She held in her hands the strong frame, the stout heart, the ruling mind. All were concentrated in Jean Letocq. He, then, must be offered up as a fitting sacrifice. By such an offering the deities could not fail to be appeased, and by the death of this man in this fashion all the natural exigencies of the situation would be satisfied. She never allowed herself to dwell for one moment on the fact that the victim was beloved by Hilda. On this point she had armed herself with bars of brass and triple steel. He might have fooled the girl, but at the thought of love her heart was ice.

The sorceress communicated her resolution to Garthmund. The chieftain exhibited no surprise: he expressed a grim approval of the proposal, which seemed likely to give an excuse for revelry and to bring the campaign to a prompt conclusion, and proceeded to make the requisite arrangements.

The 30th of March was the day chosen. The forces investing the two beleaguered positions were ordered to assemble, that on the western side on the low ground between L'Erée and Lihou, that on the northern under shelter of the woods of the Braye du Valle, facing the fortifications thrown up by the defenders. At a given signal, the kindling of a beacon on the Rocque du Guet, the two hosts were to make simultaneously a determined assault. The islanders not engaged in these operations, with the exception of those openly or secretly sympathizing with the Christians, poured into Vazon Forest, none remaining behind but those absolutely incapable of conveying themselves or of being conveyed.

By this time the consternation in the enemy's camp was all that the sorceress could desire. Jean's capture had been ascertained, and all the particulars respecting his coming fate were known by means of spies. Haco shook his head at the proposals of rescue made by spirited youths. "Success would be hopeless," he said; "failure would be fatal to those whose lives are precious to us. If he dies we will brace every nerve to avenge him, but we must be patient, and await their onslaught. Then will come our turn! then will we spring at their dastard throats! then shall they drink freely of their own gore!" If the man of the sword thought the case hopeless, what could the men of the cloister do? They did all in their power—prayed ceaselessly, fasted, did penance under the guidance of Father Austin; but nevertheless the fatal morning arrived.

Hilda knew her lover's danger. When he failed to return, and when Haco, arriving from Lihou, admitted that he had not been seen at the monastery, her heart sank; she, better than any of those around her, knew the stern, implacable patriotism and fanaticism of Judith's nature; she fully realized the savage dispositions of her countrymen, their contempt of human life, and their brutal treatment of captives. She had some conception of their fearful orgies, and she shuddered when her mind touched, not daring to dwell, on Jean's possible fate. She had sufficient presence of mind to bear up bravely before Haco, who had no suspicion that she had a perception of the terrible truth from which even his rent and seared feelings shrank; nor did she reveal to Father Austin, during a short visit which he paid her at great risk this inner serpent which was devouring her young heart. Sister Theresa and her fellows marvelled at her as on the morning of the fatal day she passed between them, her eyes rapt in contemplation, her look serene and calm, though beneath the surface lay a depth of unutterable woe, sinking, receding, chill as the dark, haunted, bosom of an unfathomable mountain lake.

She sought her own cell and begged to be left alone. Then the full heart burst the bounds imposed by the strong will. She placed before her the little Madonna, from which she never parted, and fell on her knees. She prayed till noon, and her prayer continued still; it was not simply a woman's supplication: her whole essence was poured out before the Holy Mother, who was the object of her special adoration. This girl had never known evil: for nineteen years her mind had rippled on, sparkling with good deeds, little bright thoughts, gentle inspirations sweetly obeyed; then first streamed in the warm current of human love, followed by the rapid thrilling rush of the flow of Divine awakening. The little stream had become a torrent; but one in which every element was pure, for its component parts were faith in God, trust in man, the will to act, the power to bear, contentment in joy and resignation in sorrow. Above all, she had ever before her the words which Austin had told her comprised the sermon of the universe—"Thy will be done!" Was it possible that, in the days when miracles were yet wrought, such a prayer at such a time from such a saint should not be heard? Some three hours had passed after noon when she felt a sweet languor overspread her. A mist crept before her eyes, which quickly passed away and was replaced by a radiance brighter than the sun's rays; her eyes had power however to look aloft, and she gazed with clasped hands and with loving reverence: the Holy Virgin herself stood before her, holding in her arms the Blessed Infant; the Mother looking down with a smile inexpressibly tender and compassionate, the Child stretching forth its dimpled hand and giving its blessing. She sank in rapture, the glory too great for her. As the vision faded she arose, a marvellous strength possessing her. She stepped forth, and found herself in the midst of a crowd gazing, horror-stricken, seawards. "Fear nothing," she said with a calm expression that seemed to permeate the whole assembly like an inner voice; "he is saved, and you are saved!" The words came opportunely.

## CHAPTER VII.

## ANNIHILATION.

"Prophet-like that lone one stood,
With dauntless words and high,
That shook the sere leaves from the wood
As if a storm pass'd by."

*The Last Man.*—CAMPBELL.

"So perish the old Gods!
But out of the sea of time
Rises a new land of song,
Fairer than the old."

*The Seaside and the Fireside.*—LONGFELLOW.

Full of evil augury was the morning of this eventful day in Vazon Forest. There were the same trees, the same glades and streams, as on the well-remembered Midsummer day of the preceding year; but nature and man alike were in a different mood. The trees were leafless and churlish, the glades ragged and colourless; the turbid, dusky streams bore but small resemblance to the limpid rivulets of June; the native youths were absent, engaged in military service; the maidens, headed by Suzanne Falla, had indeed an appearance of mirth, but there was a hollow ring in the boisterous recklessness of their merriment; the old men tramped feebly and aimlessly, for the reverence for age had been transferred to the veterans of the conquerors. The latter also supplied the musicians; and the clanging of drums and cymbals, with the blast of horns, replaced the sylvan melody of the aborigines.

Still there was every sign of festivity. The proceedings began with dances in which the men, who posed as athletes and warriors, gave representations of deeds of martial prowess. Then the girls were allowed to foot their native dances in their own fashion. Dances for both sexes followed, in which the native maidens found it difficult to conceal their terror of the rough partners ever ready to become rougher wooers.

These preliminaries concluded, the business of the day began. Though this wild race sacrificed human beings, they did not treat their victims with the coldblooded cruelty of the Druids, who slaughtered them as if they were oxen or sheep; their custom was to burn their captives; and it is not for critics, whose pious forefathers kindled the fires of Smithfield, to assert that their practice was wholly barbarous. In the present case a pyre, some twelve feet high, was built at the foot of a huge granite boulder, near the sea-coast: it was constructed of dry wood, and was drenched with combustible materials. Jean was bound firmly to a strong hurdle, made of birch stems and withies securely lashed together. Judith, Garthmund, and the principal elders, placed themselves under the venerable oak; the people stood at a respectful distance. Twelve stalwart warriors bore the litter on which the prisoner was stretched, and placed it on stone trestles planted for the purpose in the intervening space. Then the priests arrived; twelve old men whose white locks and beards, and snowy dresses, gave them a venerable appearance which was soon belied by their performances.

Halting when they reached the victim, the priests faced the oak, and chanted a solemn, wailing dirge; this, which might have been a farewell to the spirit whose departure they were preparing to accelerate, was not unimpressive. Then one stepped forward whose voice was yet clear and loud; he passed a warm eulogy on the qualities of the captive, whom he described in exaggerated phrases as a sage in council, and a hero in battle, endowing him also with every domestic virtue which seemed in his eyes worthy of enumeration. This discourse was followed by a warlike song in honour of Thor and Odin, and it was during the course of this hymn that it became clear from their rolling eyes and unsteady gait that the old men were in a state of no ordinary excitement. All night they had been feasting their deities, and the solemnity had involved deep potations; now, as the rapid movements of a dance which accompanied the inspiriting words sent the fumes into their heads, they appeared to be beside themselves. The bystanders, however, attributing their frenzy to religious fervour, and not unaccustomed to such manifestations, looked on unmoved. The music ceased; and the song of triumph gave way to a hideous scene over which it were painful to dwell. The drunken old men, with incredible agility, whirled round the prostrate form of Jean. There was no question now of eulogizing his virtues: he was accused, in language which seemed devil-born, of every crime, every infamy, of which the human race is capable; held up to scorn and ignominy, he was cursed and execrated with a shower of blasphemy and obscenity; a by-stander, contemplating his calm, clear face, the lips parted in prayer, gleaming amidst the contorted features of the screaming miscreants, might have believed him to be already passing, unscathed, through the terrors of purgatory.

It is impossible at this day to fathom the mystery of this terrible relic of some remote superstition. It may have been that the abhorrence and extinction of evil was roughly typified, or that it was understood that the death of the victim would, as if he were a scapegoat, cleanse the worshippers of the sins with which he was thus loaded. It is idle to grope where all is, and must be, dark; all that can be asserted with any certainty is that the preliminary eulogy, a more modern practice, was intended to enhance the value of the offering which they were about to make to the Gods.

The warriors now resumed their burden, and a procession was formed towards the pyre, on which the litter-bearers, mounting by an inclined plane, placed the doomed youth. Judith ascended the huge boulder, which was some eight feet higher than the pyre at its foot. The chief and people grouped themselves round its base. The priests stood ready to apply the torch when the sorceress gave the signal, and the distant watchman on the Guct waited in his turn for the first flash of flame to kindle the beacon which was to set the assailing forces in motion.

Judith turned to the expectant crowd: her glance was searching, in her eye was an ineffable look of scorn. "Down on your knees!" she said, "craven sons, whose sires would blush to own you! You who have steeped your hearts in pride and boastfulness! Were your fathers slow to draw the sword and quick to sheathe it? Did they cower by their hearths when warm blood was being spilt? did they feast when others fought? would they not have leaped, as the tempest rushes from its caves, to scatter like the sand those who should have dared to bend the knee to false Gods, objects of their loathing and derision? Runs this noble blood in your stagnant veins? From giants ye have become pigmies!" The majestic contempt with which these words had been delivered had a crushing effect. She continued her harangue for some time in the same strain. Every Voizin's head was bowed, every form bent and trembling. The sorceress then, slowly turning, faced seaward. Her arms assumed the well-known beseeching attitude, the serpent bracelet glittering fiercely in the sun. Her voice changed, became softer. "Yet they are my people!" she continued, "and the last of our race. Ennoble them, great Gods! quicken their hearts and spare them!" Looking outward with the rapt look of a prophetess in whom, though torn with tempests of fanaticism and of passion, human and superhuman, no thought was mean, no sentiment ignoble, she poured out this her prayer; not for mercy!—her Gods knew not this attribute; nor could she understand it; if the craven continued to be a craven she felt he were better dead;—not for peace and contentment!—to these blessings neither she nor they attached value;—but for fearlessness and steadfastness of purpose, and also for courage to die for the truth! there were petitions poured out by this woman that would have honoured the lips of the champion of any creed.

The supplication ended, she seemed about to raise her hand to give the anticipated signal when a look of amazement passed over her features; she brushed her hand over her eyes and looked again, then folded her arms and gazed steadily seawards. What she saw might have shattered even her nerves of iron. At the close of her prayer, which had exactly coincided with the moment when Hilda stepped from her cell, the bosom of the sea heaved and rose: a wave, ten feet high, glided, stole as it were, so gently did it move, into the forest; but so rapidly, that in one minute every human being except herself and Jean was engulphed. They were gone, the high-couraged and the craven, the frenzied priest and the laughing child, with their passions, their hopes, and their fears, without the faintest note of warning of coming danger! Judith glanced at Jean, almost contemptuously; he, not having seen what had happened, was still momentarily expecting the application of the torch. A second wave crept in, smaller than the former, but overwhelming the pyre. The dazed warrior on the Guet reported that after this second wave had passed he saw the tall form still towering on the peak, but that when he looked again the rock, though still above water, was tenantless; a little later the granite mass, together with the tops of the tallest trees, lay under an unruffled surface.

When the pyre was submerged the litter, to which Jean was attached, floated off and formed a tolerably secure raft. His life was safe for a time; but he would have been exposed to a still more ghastly fate from the swooping sea-birds had he not been able by a supreme effort to wrest one of his arms from its bands. In speechless wonderment he was carried seaward by the slowly receding tide. Suddenly his raft was hailed by a well-known voice. Friendly hands cut the ropes that bound him, and he was lifted into a boat. The occupant was Haco who, attracted to the spot when hurrying to the Vale, by the cries of the clustering gulls, had thus again saved his life.

The giant pulled vigorously to the point which, now known as the Hommet, terminates the northern arm of Vazon Bay; there he landed the youth, to enable him to stretch his cramped limbs, and to clothe him in such articles as he could spare from his own equipment. A rapid explanation passed between them. Haco told him how the force investing Lihou had, when apparently waiting for a signal to move, been overwhelmed by a wave which cut off the promontory from L'Erée, and had perished to a man. Jean could tell of nothing but the sudden cessation of the tumult and the floating of his litter. The minds of both were wandering, burningly anxious as they were to know what had passed at the Vale. Scaling the Hommet, they obtained a sufficient view to satisfy them that Lancresse Common no longer formed a portion of the mainland; an hour afterwards, entering the Grand Havre, they saw an unbroken channel between that inlet and St. Sampson's: every trace of the invading host had disappeared. Jean was soon in Hilda's arms; and the two lovers, with Haco, spent the remainder of the day in pious thanksgiving to the Holy Mother by whose special interposition, testified so miraculously to the maiden, the cause of Christ had triumphed and the parted had been reunited, when the last gleam of safety seemed to have been extinguished.

The next morning Father Austin arrived. Hilda was then made acquainted with her relationship to Haco, whose tender attentions during her late troubles had already won her unreserved affection. The news was an inexpressible joy to her, and it was touching to see how she nestled in the deep embrace of her father, whose feelings, so long pent up, now at last found vent. Jean absented himself during the day, but on the following morning insisted that his nuptials should no longer be deferred. The same evening, in the little chapel of the nunnery, Austin bestowed his blessing on a union which had been sanctified by such special manifestations of Divine approval.

The readjustment of the shattered organization of the island was imperative. The inhabitants of the eastern side, and those of the Vale, had for the most part preserved their lives by their absence from the forest; the Christian converts who had aided in the struggle were also safe; with these exceptions the island was practically depopulated. Jean was elected chief by acclamation. After giving such pressing directions as immediate exigencies required, he acceded to his wife's ardent wish to obtain intelligence respecting Judith, and also to ascertain the fate of Tita.

The Lihou monks had already reported that all communication was broken between the Hanois and the shore, but that the tower appeared to be intact. On an April morning Haco and the young couple sailed across Rocquaine Bay, and landed close to the tower, which now stood on a rugged and inhospitable island. The door was opened by Tita, who smiled, and prattled, and caressed her young mistress like a lap-dog. She recognised Jean with indifference, but a start, followed by a shudder, seized her when she observed Haco; her terror, however, seemed to pass away when he spoke a few soothing words to her. It was evident that a shock, or a succession of shocks, had unsettled the poor woman's brain. On the name of Judith being mentioned, she pointed fearfully to the upper story. Uncertain as to her meaning, Jean cautiously ascended the ladder, and ascertained that the sorceress was in truth there. After a consultation it was decided that Haco and Hilda should seek her presence.

As father and daughter entered the apartment, they saw the old woman half-seated, half-lying, on a couch placed close to the window; her face, which was turned seaward, was haggard, the leanness bringing into strong relief the handsome chiselling of her profile; the sternness of her mouth was somewhat relaxed; there was an indication almost of softness in its corners. Her high spirit had accepted, not resented, defeat.

As her eye fell on her two visitors there was no gleam of defiance, no mark of anger, or even surprise; but, when Haco stood fully revealed before her, a flash of triumph and pleasure shot into it, kindling every feature with its glow. "You here, Haco!" she cried, "and with her! The Gods have relented. You will hold her fast in their worship, and lead her steps to the land of her sires! I die contented." She fell back exhausted. "Sister," said the giant, laying his hand softly on her shoulder, "it is too late; when Algar slew my loved one the Pagan died in me; I am a servant of the God of the Christians." Hilda awaited fearfully the result of this announcement, but she knew not the greatness of the old woman's soul. It was long ere her voice was heard again. Presently, raising herself, she said, "I would it had been otherwise; but I have erred, I have misjudged. I thought that your Gods were false; puny creations of a nerveless brain; but they are strong, I own their power! It may be that the great ones of old have wearied of our spiritless race, and abandoned us. So perchance you may be wise to turn to the new-comers!" Her voice failed her, but as they knelt by her side her hands wandered over their heads and lingered with a caressing movement among Hilda's locks. She seemed to have forgotten Jean, whom she doubtless believed to have been lost in the general calamity. Suddenly she started up and pointed to a storm-cloud rising rapidly from the western horizon, assuming a succession of fantastic shapes as it passed upwards. "Do you not see them?" she cried—"the great, the glorious ones! they bend from their seats; they smile! see their power! Their majesty! their locks stream, their swords are half drawn! they sheathe them, they lean forward, they extend their arms! they beckon!—I come, I come!" She stretched out her arms with the old familiar gesture and sank back, having breathed her spirit to the tempest which she loved so well.

52

Guernsey, Eastern Side, with Islands of Herm, Jethou and Sark.
Sketched in 1839.

They buried her on the cliffs of Pleinmont, where a cairn long marked her resting-place. Tita was taken to the Vale; all attempts to restore her from the shock which her nerves had received failed till on one sunny morning Hilda's infant was placed on her knees: when the child crowed, and smiled at her, the cloud imperceptibly passed away, never to return. From that time she assumed her regular place in the household.

Haco abandoned his Lihou cell; his rough readiness of resource, unfailing good-humour, and skill in managing men, proved invaluable during the task of the restoration of the broken links of government and society.

The labours of Father Austin and his coadjutors did not relax, but their course lay in smoother waters: if their prospects of martyrdom were diminished they were more than consoled by the knowledge that they possessed among them a veritable saint, to whom the Holy Virgin had vouchsafed the honour of a personal appearance, and that they had been witnesses of a miraculous interposition, the evidence of which would be indelible as long as the sea should wash the storm-beaten cliffs of their beloved island.